Praise for
THE MARCHING BAND NERDS HANDBOOK

"From the 13th Chair Trombone Player, a fun and insightful look at the crazy world of marching band! DJ Corchin has done it again. Through his 'rules,' DJ takes the activity we love and shows us measure by measure why we love it. I declare *The Marching Band Nerds Handbook* to be required reading for all incoming band freshmen. (Also seniors, parents, directors, administrators, and...well, you get where I'm going here...) Go for it... Break ranks!"

—Chuck Henson, the "Voice" of Bands of America

"DJ does it again! Band nerds of all ages will enjoy the humorous, thoughtful, and clever lessons presented in the book. Witty illustrations by Dan Dougherty add an extra level of value."

—Courtney Brandt, author of the Line series
and *Confessions of a Teenage Band Geek*

The MARCHING BAND NERDS

Handbook

RULES FROM THE 13TH CHAIR TROMBONE PLAYER

DJ CORCHIN

ILLUSTRATED BY DAN DOUGHERTY

sourcebooks
eXplore

Dedicated to

T.S.

From the outside looking in, no one understands it.
From the inside looking out, no one can explain it.

Published by Sourcebooks eXplore, an imprint of Sourcebooks Kids
P.O. Box 4410, Naperville, Illinois 60567-4410
(630) 961-3900
sourcebookskids.com

Originally published in 2012 in the United States of America by The phazelFOZ Company, LLC.

Library of Congress Cataloging-in-Publication data is on file with the publisher.

Printed and bound in the United States of America.
VP 10 9 8 7 6 5 4 3 2 1

FUN

Fun is the greatest luxury of our time. It's become our way of reward-
ing ourselves after the real "important things" are taken care of. Having
fun, although we like to say it's important, is extremely underrated. Fun
should be the supercharged, nuclear, cosmic fuel that can power the world
toward the way we always hoped it to be. If more people were having fun,
there would be no reason for hate or discrimination or any other evil.
Regardless of your world and social views the truth remains: evil is not
fun, good is fun. Fun is inclusive, loving, humorous, healing, and every-
thing else that moves us forward. To all the people who are slowing us
down…lighten up. Grab a cupcake and chill out. The world's lost a bit of
its will to have fun. To me, that's dumb. I don't want to be dumb.

Treat others how you want to be treated.

It's a salute, not interpretive dance.

Every day is a deodorant day.

Never put a freshman on water duty.

Never put a senior on water duty.

"Dress right" has two meanings.
Both equally important.

Band parents mean well.

Passion is good.

Compassion is better.

Don't lock your knees when standing at attention.

Revenge is sweet.

Be careful of what you post online.

Don't let the guard lead stretches.

Technology can enhance the show...

...except in the rain.

Trombone slides are not lightsabers.

Don't worry about what's going on in the back of the bus.
It's better you don't know.

Live animals are not a good
idea for any show.

Trumpets: calm down.

Being in charge of the metronome ain't so bad.

When life seems too big to overcome,
slow it down, take one measure
at a time, and subdivide.

BAND NERDS

Pay-Attention-To-Us-At-A-Football-Game Kit

1. Foghorn
2. Six foot gigantic trophy w/ movable cart
3. Bikinis for the band
4. ...EVERYONE in the band
5. T-shirt rocket launcher
6. Hometown reality pop star
7. Emergency Earth, Wind & Fire music
8. A backbeat
9. A backflip to a backbeat while back'n that thang up
10. Eight gigantic drums in the front
11. A cute puppy

Never give drummers metal sticks.
They think they're ninjas.

But most ninjas are clarinet players.

Band parents *are* adults.
But that doesn't mean they don't need supervision.

What happens in sectionals,
stays in sectionals.

Don't be "that person" during the company front.

No energy drinks before the show.

If you get a flute solo...rock it.

There's something to be said for being a nerd.

Seriously, no more fire
out of the tuba bell.

Toes up...

'cause ya never know.

Pyramids don't work in marching band.

Use a special mellophone mouthpiece when possible.
It makes it easier to stay on your face.

Let the uniform parents do their job.
They probably know best.

Never try to make a French horn–shaped formation.
It's just too confusing.

Law of the jungle: serve or be served.

Directors can wear T-shirts and shorts during rehearsals.

Never run with a piccolo.

Always run with a sousaphone.

Be nice to alternates. You never know when they'll be your drum major.

PUSH-UP LIST FOR WHEN I'M DRUM MAJOR
1. ROBERT
2. BECKY
3. ROBERT Two
4. NICKY
5. SHANNON
6. AMY
7.

Earn respect. Don't demand it.

Marching band is an art, not a sport.

But if it were a sport, the drummers would win.

Make sure to respect your elders.

They need it in today's day and age.

Don't expect too much from saxes during a horn flash.

Don't expect *anything* from baritones.

Use the force.

It's easier on the back.

Practice 8 to 5 whenever you can.

But not 24 to 5.

There is such a thing as overperforming.

As cool as gauntlets are, they should only be
worn during band performances.

Invest in a full-length mirror.

Take what you do seriously.

But don't take yourself too seriously.

Always make sure the bari sax player
is taller than the instrument.

Give the announcer the phonetic spellings.

There's a reason bassoons don't march.

If you make a mistake...sell it.

Don't cut the band's funding.

It's not a pretty sight.

Wear the right color socks.

Cheese fundraisers are not a
good idea in the summer.

Beauty is in the eye of the beholder.

A real piano is too much for band parents.

Don't take "pit" literally.

Clarinets, don't worry.
Someone, somewhere, hears you.

Having the band dance is cool.

Just don't forget about your instruments.

Angels don't have a favorite instrument.
They love everyone.

On the other hand...

Never serve sushi before a competition.

Flutes, be sure to work out your left shoulder too.

Some things aren't meant to be tossed.

Hockey and band DO have something in common.

Listen to your section leader.
Your life may depend on it.

Bring a bigger blanket.

Be sure to think about any pass-throughs
before running the drill.

The performance is a celebration of all
your hard work, not the culmination of it.

Don't use rubber sticks.

Balloons are not a good idea.

Go to the bathroom BEFORE practice.

On your first day, ask more questions
instead of knowing all the answers.

Make sure people can understand your show.

Size doesn't matter...much.

If a judge gets in your way, keep marching.

Just make sure it's not right before a halt.

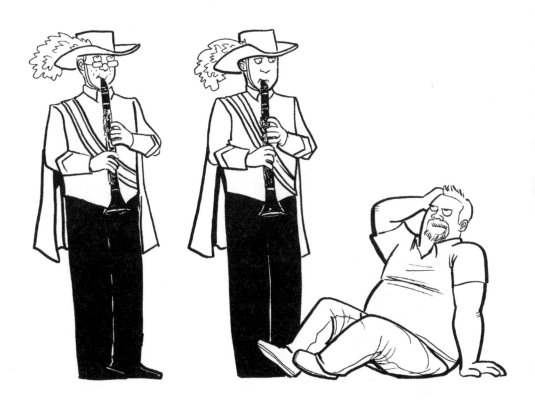

Never lick your horn before a cold night performance.

Actually, never lick your horn.
That's just weird.

Teach the parents the appropriate
time to applaud.

Stay hydrated.
Rehearsal in the heat is hot.

Color guard's famous last words:
"Trust me."

Make sure to mic the oboe solo.
They just can't handle fortissimo.

Don't judge a book by its cover.

Judge it by its spine.

Stick to the basics at the concession stand.

If it's windy, don't toss.

Sometimes props can be too much.

Don't fight among yourselves.

When designing the guard costumes, keep
in mind the month of November.

It's a podium, not a studio apartment.

Never use Velcro shoes.

Don't forget to turn off the mic.

Only fart during the loud parts.
That's what the *f* stands for.

That includes the audience.

The Unscalable Wall

My marching band and I reached an unscalable wall.
We tried to climb over, but it's impossibly tall.
It's a million feet wide and a billion yards up.
We tried to march through it, but that wasn't enough.

There were words on the wall that were scattered about.
Words like *difficult*, *impossible*, *fear*, and *self-doubt*.
Sometimes we'd feel like we wanted to quit.
That the wall was much bigger than we'd like to admit.

But we'd pick ourselves up and break down our parts.
We'd drill in our moves 'til we knew them by heart.
The judges would judge us show after show,
The wall's shadow upon us wherever we'd go.

But when Finals arrived, the words were not taunting.
The wall was still there, but it wasn't as daunting.
In the end, it was us the audience crowned.
We made a wall of our own, a wall of our sound.

PEACE WITH A WHOLE LOTTA HAIR GREASE.

SEE YA. ♩♪

A Special Band Nerds Thank-You to

Jessica

Mom

Scott

Chance

Meg

Kevin

Greg

Bimm

Courtney Brandt

Ben Harloff

Chuck Henson

Jeff Handel

Ken Martinson

Amy McCabe

Jason Wick

DJ CORCHIN, otherwise known in the band world as the 13th Chair, has been involved in music education since learning to play the viola in third grade. And by learning, he means immediately forgetting how to play it the following year when he started on trombone. Growing up in the band world, DJ graduated from DePaul University in Chicago with a degree in music education and immediately did not use it. Instead, he became a featured performer riding a unicycle and playing the trombone in the Tony and Emmy Award–winning Broadway show, *Blast!*, as one does. Shortly after, he became a high school band director developing band nerds for future world domination. When a takeover didn't materialize, he started a career as a children's author writing books about kindness and communication. As one does.

COLLECT ALL THE
BAND NERDS
BOOKS!

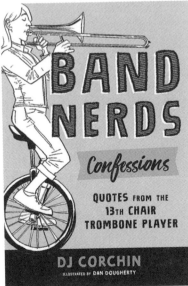